DESERTS
THIRSTY WONDERLANDS

by Laura Purdie Salas

illustrated by Jeff Yesh

Thanks to our advisers for their expertise, research, and advice:

Michael T. Lares, Ph.D., Associate Professor of Biology
University of Mary, Bismarck, North Dakota

Susan Kesselring, M.A., Literacy Educator
Rosemount–Apple Valley–Eagan (Minnesota) School District

PICTURE WINDOW BOOKS
Minneapolis, Minnesota

Editor: Jill Kalz

Designers: Joe Anderson and Hilary Wacholz

Page Production: Angela Kilmer

Art Director: Nathan Gassman

Associate Managing Editor: Christianne Jones

The illustrations in this book were created digitally.

Picture Window Books

5115 Excelsior Boulevard

Suite 232

Minneapolis, MN 55416

877-845-8392

www.picturewindowbooks.com

Printed in the United States of America.

Library of Congress Cataloging-in-Publication Data

Salas, Laura Purdie.

Deserts : thirsty wonderlands / by Laura Purdie Salas ; illustrated by Jeff Yesh.

p. cm. – (Amazing science)

Includes bibliographical references and index.

ISBN-13: 978-1-4048-3095-0 (library binding)

ISBN-10: 1-4048-3095-2 (library binding)

ISBN-13: 978-1-4048-3469-9 (paperback)

ISBN-10: 1-4048-3469-9 (paperback)

1. Deserts—Juvenile literature. I. Yesh, Jeff, 1971- ill. II. Title.

QH88.S25 2007

577.54–dc22   2006027830

Table of Contents

Very Little Water

Do you live in a place that gets less than 10 inches (25 centimeters) of rain per year? If you do, you probably live in a desert! A desert is a dry ecosystem. An ecosystem is all of the living and nonliving things in a certain area. It includes plants, animals, water, soil, weather … everything!

FUN FACT

Not all deserts are sandy and hot. Most deserts are rocky.
And some deserts are cold. Instead of rain, they get snow!

Deserts All Over the World

North America

South America

Deserts cover about one-fifth of Earth's land. The largest sand or rock desert is the Sahara Desert in Africa. All 48 states of the mainland United States could fit in the Sahara.

Other large deserts in the world include the Arabian Desert, the Australian Desert, and the Gobi Desert.

DESERTS

Asia

Europe

Arabian
Desert

Gobi
Desert

Sahara
Desert

EQUATOR

Africa

Australian
Desert

Australia

FUN FACT

The frozen continent of Antarctica is a special kind of desert. It
holds 90 percent of the world's ice. But because that ice never
melts, there is no liquid water. Antarctica is a very dry ecosystem,
so it's called a desert.

Antarctica

Extreme Weather

Most deserts are hot and cold. The sun bakes the desert during the day. But the air has no water to trap the sun's heat. So, when the sun sets, the desert turns cold. The temperature can drop 60 degrees Fahrenheit (16 degrees Celsius) at night!

Deserts have extreme weather. Sometimes, heavy rains cause floods. Very strong winds cause sandstorms.

FUN FACT

Wind makes sand dunes. As the wind blows, it picks up sand. When the wind hits a plant or other object, it slows down and drops some of its sand. Sand builds up around the object. This happens over and over. After a long time, a sand dune forms.

Plants: How They Get Water

How can plants grow with little water? Desert plants soak up and store water in their cells. Barrel cactuses spread their roots wide. They soak up rainfall from all around the plant. Mesquite trees have long roots. The roots find water deep under the ground.

Many desert plants store water inside their cells. Cactuses and other plants called succulents have waxy skins that hold water in.

PLANT CELLS

FUN FACT

The tall saguaro cactus can hold hundreds of gallons
of water. Like other desert plants, it has sharp thorns.
Thorns help keep animals from pecking at the plants
for a drink.

Plants: Waiting for the Rain

Some desert plants do not store water. They just wait for rain. Daisies, desert peas, and lilies are a few of these. Their seeds lie in the soil and wait for rain. Some seeds can live in the ground for years.

After the rain, the seeds grow quickly into plants. The desert bursts with color for a couple weeks. Then the plants die. But their seeds lie in the ground, waiting for the next rain.

BRINE SHRIMP

FUN FACT

Like many desert plants, some desert animals do not come alive
until it rains. Tiny brine shrimp live in salt lakes. During dry periods,
the lakes dry up. The shrimp die, but their eggs do not. The eggs
can stay alive for many years—in some cases, up to 100 years!
When it finally rains, the eggs hatch within two days.

Animals: Getting Water

Like desert plants, desert animals also must get and store water. Lizards and snakes have thick skin that holds in water. Some kinds of beetles and other animals drink morning dew.

Some antelopes get all of their water from eating water-filled plants. Falcons and hawks get their water from the animals they eat.

FUN FACT

It is hard for most large mammals to live in the desert. They cannot store water, and their fur traps heat. Cheetahs and lions are examples of large mammals that have adapted to life in the desert.

15

Animals: Staying Cool

Many insects, reptiles, and small mammals live in the desert. They adapt to the heat in different ways. For example, the fennec fox and the jackrabbit have huge ears. The animals' body heat travels out through their ears. Cougars, bighorn sheep, and many other animals have light-colored fur. Light colors absorb less heat from the sun than dark colors.

Many desert animals are nocturnal. They sleep under the ground during the hot day. They are awake during the cool night.

FUN FACT

Some desert animals move in special ways so the hot sand does not burn them. Sidewinder snakes whip along so their bodies do not touch much sand. The fringe-toed lizard holds its head and body up off the sand. Chameleons let only two feet at a time touch the sand.

The Spreading Desert

Earth's deserts are growing.

Imagine a place that's not a desert. Now, suppose people eat all of the plants. They chop down all of the trees. The wind blows away the soil because there are no plant roots to hold it. This land might eventually turn into a desert. The original plants and animals would not be able to survive in the new desert.

FUN FACT

Desertification happened in the United States during the 1930s. Dry weather and poor farming methods turned Kansas and several other states into a desert-like place. Wind blew dust into huge dust storms. The area became known as the Dust Bowl.

Gifts of the Desert

Deserts are full of gifts. They give homes to many animals and plants. People mine silver and gold from below the desert floor. They find oil there to make gasoline. They use certain desert plants in medicines. But deserts are also very fragile ecosystems. Once people disturb them, deserts take a long time to recover.

Deserts are valuable places, but it's important to protect Earth's other ecosystems, too. Each has its own special gifts. Together, Earth's ecosystems make the planet a wonderful place to live!

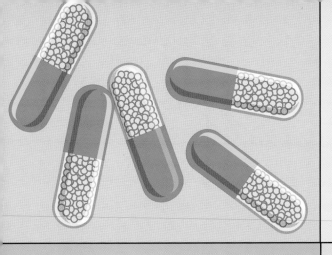

FUN FACT

People use many things that come from desert plants. Some soaps have jojoba oil in them. The oil comes from the jojoba plant, which lives in the desert. Scientists also make medicines from desert plants such as yucca and mesquite plants.

Desert Diorama: Desert in a Box

WHAT YOU NEED:

- a shoebox
- self-drying modeling clay
- glue
- sand
- scissors
- colored paper
- pictures of desert plants and animals

WHAT YOU DO:

1. First, turn the shoebox on its side.

2. Use self-drying modeling clay to build sand dunes inside the shoebox.

3. After the sand dunes dry, spread a very thin layer of glue over them. Then sprinkle sand over the glue, and let it dry. Shake off the extra sand.

4. Now, create your desert scene. Sandy deserts often have cactus plants or palm trees. They might have jackrabbits, foxes, and snakes. Use colored paper, clay, or pictures to make the plants and animals of the desert ecosystem. Then glue them onto your sand dunes. Be creative!

Desert Facts

- The hottest and coldest temperatures on Earth were measured in deserts. In 1922, it was 136° F (58° C) in the Sahara Desert. In 1983, it was 129° F below zero (89° C below zero) in Antarctica.

- The Atacama Desert of northern Chile gets less than 0.3 inches (8 millimeters) of rain each year. That's not even as tall as the eraser at the end of your pencil. Atacama is the driest place on Earth.

- People in the African deserts raise camels to carry things. Camels are often called "ships of the desert." They roll and rock when they run. Riding a camel can feel like sailing on the ocean.

- An oasis is a place in the desert with water, plants, and trees. The water comes from very old rivers that run deep below the desert. Sometimes a river comes to a big crack in the rocks. Then the water flows up along the crack until it reaches the surface.

Glossary

adapt—to change in order to improve one's chances for survival

cells—basic parts of animals or plants that are so small you can't see them without a microscope

desertification—the process by which land that is not desert slowly turns into desert

ecosystem—an area with certain animals, plants, weather, and land or water features

extreme—beyond the usual

mammals—warm-blooded animals that feed their young milk

reptiles—cold-blooded animals with a backbone and scales

succulents—plants with a tough skin and thick, heavy leaves or stems; cactuses and aloe are examples of succulents

To Learn More

AT THE LIBRARY

Gaff, Jackie. *I Wonder Why the Sahara Is Cold at Night: And Other Questions About the Deserts.* New York: Kingfisher, 2004.

Johnson, Rebecca L., and Phyllis V. Saroff. *A Walk in the Desert.* Minneapolis: Carolrhoda Books, 2001.

Wilkins, Sally. *Deserts.* Mankato, Minn.: Bridgestone Books, 2001.

ON THE WEB

FactHound offers a safe, fun way to find Web sites related to this book. All of the sites on FactHound have been researched by our staff.

1. Visit *www.facthound.com*
2. Type in this special code: 1404830952
3. Click on the FETCH IT button.

Your trusty FactHound will fetch the best sites for you!

Index

LOOK FOR ALL OF THE BOOKS IN THE AMAZING SCIENCE– ECOSYSTEMS SERIES:

Deserts: Thirsty Wonderlands

Grasslands: Fields of Green and Gold

Oceans: Underwater Worlds

Rain Forests: Gardens of Green

Temperate Deciduous Forests: Lands of Falling Leaves

Wetlands: Soggy Habitat